W9-CGP-791

THE C-WORD

Avon, Massachusetts

Copyright © 2012 by F+W Media, Inc.
All rights reserved.
This book, or parts thereof, may not be reproduced in any
form without permission from the publisher; exceptions are
made for brief excerpts used in published reviews.

Published by
Adams Media, a division of F+W Media, Inc.
57 Littlefield Street, Avon, MA 02322. U.S.A.
www.adamsmedia.com

ISBN 10: 1-4405-4359-3
ISBN 13: 978-1-4405-4359-3
eISBN 10: 1-4405-4360-7
eISBN 13: 978-1-4405-4360-9

Printed in the United States of America.

10   9   8   7   6   5   4   3   2

This publication is designed to provide accurate and authoritative information with regard to the subject matter covered. It is sold with the understanding that the publisher is not engaged in rendering legal, accounting, or other professional advice. If legal advice or other expert assistance is required, the services of a competent professional person should be sought.

—From a *Declaration of Principles* jointly adopted by a Committee of the American Bar Association and a Committee of Publishers and Associations

Photographs © istock.com and 123rf.com.

This book is available at quantity discounts for bulk purchases.
For information, please call 1-800-289-0963.

P. 1: 123rf.com © Dmitry Kalinovsky
P. 2: 123rf.com © jirkaejc
P. 3: 123rf.com © Anna Yakimova
P. 4: 123rf.com © Eric IsselÃƒÂ©e
P. 5: istockphoto.com © tunart
P. 6: 123rf.com © Gallo Gusztav
P. 7: 123rf.com © natulrich
P. 8: 123rf.com © Sarah Fields
P. 9: 123rf.com © anyka
P. 10-11: 123rf.com © Roman Milert
P. 12: 123rf.com © Viorel Sima
P. 13: 123rf.com © Ferenc Szelepcsenyi
P. 14: 123rf.com © Eric IsselÃƒÂ©e
P. 15: 123rf.com © Anna Yakimova
P. 16: 123rf.com © Achim Prill
P. 17: 123rf.com © Anthony Vodak
P. 18: 123rf.com © Andrey Bourdioukov
P. 19: 123rf.com © Olga Miltsova
P. 20: 123rf.com © Morozova Tatiana
P. 21: 123rf.com © sthompson407
P. 22: 123rf.com © Anna Yakimova
P. 23: 123rf.com © Ramona Smiers
P. 24: 123rf.com © Eric IsselÃƒÂ©e
P. 25: 123rf.com © Miroslava Arnaudova
P. 26: istockphoto.com © Kyoungil Jeon
P. 27: clipart.com
P. 28: 123rf.com © anyka
P. 29: 123rf.com © Martine Oger
P. 30: 123rf.com © digifuture
P. 31: istockphoto.com © Jonny
Kristoffersson
P. 32: 123rf.com © flib
P. 33: 123rf.com © Ferenc Szelepcsenyi
P. 34: 123rf.com © Odelia Cohen
P. 35: 123rf.com © Ferenc Szelepcsenyi
P. 36: 123rf.com © Ekaterina Fribus
P. 37: istockphoto.com © Tony Campbell
P. 38: 123rf.com © digifuture
P. 39: istockphoto.com © TERADAT
SANTIVIVUT
P. 40: 123rf.com © TATIANA MAKOTRA
P. 41: 123rf.com © Anna Yakimova
P. 42: 123rf.com © ЯÑ„Ð½Ð°
ÐœÐ°Ð¼Ð¾Ñ‡ÐºÐ¸Ð½Ð°
P. 43: istockphoto.com © Ira Bachinskaya
P. 44: 123rf.com © Walter Arce
P. 45: 123rf.com © Ramon Espelt
Gorgozo
P. 46: 123rf.com © cherrymerry
P. 47: 123rf.com © Georgi Pavlov
P. 48: 123rf.com © Anna Utekhina
P. 49: istockphoto.com © BrAt_PiKaChU
P. 50: 123rf.com © Lucy Baldwin
P. 51: 123rf.com © Mikhail Dudarev
P. 52: 123rf.com © Ljupco Smokovski
P. 53: 123rf.com © photopm
P. 54: 123rf.com © anytka
P. 55: 123rf.com © Anna Yakimova
P. 56: 123rf.com © Ali Peterson
P. 57: 123rf.com © Bonzami Emmanuelle

P. 58: 123rf.com © anytka
P. 59: 123rf.com © Andriy Solovyov
P. 60: 123rf.com © Pashkov Andrey
P. 61: 123rf.com © Evgeniya Uvarova
P. 62: 123rf.com © Katrina Brown
P. 63: 123rf.com © Rafal Olkis
P. 64: istockphoto.com © Sue Loader
P. 65: 123rf.com © satina
P. 66: istockphoto.com © Andrey Kuzmin
P. 67: istockphoto.com © Michelle Gibson
P. 68: 123rf.com © Anna Yakimova
P. 69: 123rf.com © natika
P. 70: 123rf.com © Roksana Bashyrova
P. 71: istockphoto.com © Waltraud Ingerl
P. 72: istockphoto.com © Vitaly Titov
P. 73: istockphoto.com © Vladimir
Suponev
P. 74: istockphoto.com © Anna Utekhina
P. 75: 123rf.com © Eric IsselÃƒÂ©e
P. 76: 123rf.com © kho
P. 77: 123rf.com © jojobob
P. 78: 123rf.com © Liliya Kulianionak
P. 79: 123rf.com © Vladimir Suponev
P. 80: istockphoto.com © max homand
P. 81: istockphoto.com © Kjell Brynildsen
P. 82: istockphoto.com © Tony Campbell
P. 83: istockphoto.com © Tony Campbell
P. 84: istockphoto.com © Nicole S. Young
P. 85: 123rf.com © mermozine
P. 86: istockphoto.com © kimeveruss
P. 87: istockphoto.com © Michael
Westhoff
P. 88: 123rf.com © Galyna Andrushko
P. 89: istockphoto.com ©
foodandwinephotography
P. 90: 123rf.com © Anatoliy Samara
P. 91: 123rf.com © Anna Yakimova
P. 92: 123rf.com © TATIANA MAKOTRA
P. 93: 123rf.com © Vladimir Voronin
P. 94: 123rf.com © Andrey Bourdioukov
P. 95: 123rf.com © anytka
P. 96: istockphoto.com © Tatiana
Morozova
P. 97: 123rf.com © Daria Minaeva
P. 98: clipart.com
P. 99: istockphoto.com © Hande Guleryuz
Yuce
P. 100: istockphoto.com © Tony Campbell
P. 101: istockphoto.com © Tomas Petura
P. 102: istockphoto.com © Katarzyna
Mazurowska
P. 103: 123rf.com © Nailia Schwarz
P. 104: 123rf.com © Vitaly Titov
P. 105: 123rf.com © Nailia Schwarz
P. 106: istockphoto.com © Mariya
Bibikova
P. 107: 123rf.com © Jakub Gojda
P. 108: istockphoto.com ©
clearstockconcepts
P. 109: 123rf.com © Anna Yakimova

P. 110: istockphoto.com © johanna
goodyear
P. 111: istockphoto.com © Mehmet Salih
Guler
P. 112: 123rf.com © aivolie
P. 113: istockphoto.com © Erik Khalitov
P. 114: 123rf.com © Visarute
Angkatavanich
P. 115: 123rf.com © Anna Yakimova
P. 116: 123rf.com © Andrey Kuzmin
P. 117: 123rf.com © PaylessImages
P. 118: 123rf.com © Viorel Sima
P. 119: 123rf.com © Anthony Vodak
P. 120: 123rf.com © Jeffrey Van Daele
P. 121: 123rf.com © Serghei Velusceac
P. 122: 123rf.com © Karin Lau
P. 123: istockphoto.com © Stig Andersen
P. 124: clipart.com
P. 125: 123rf.com © Jim Lopes
P. 126: 123rf.com © Michael Pettigrew
P. 127: 123rf.com © Sara Robinson
P. 128: istockphoto.com © DenGuy
P. 129: 123rf.com © Anna Yakimova
P. 130: 123rf.com © Vladyslav
Starozhylov
P. 131: istockphoto.com © Mehmet Salih
Guler
P. 132: 123rf.com © Sergiu Bacioiu
P. 133: 123rf.com © Pavel Timofeev
P. 134: 123rf.com © Simone Van Den
Berg
P. 135: istockphoto.com © Patrick Duffy
P. 136: 123rf.com © sharyfox
P. 137: 123rf.com © Alexey Ukhov
P. 138: 123rf.com © Sergey Kouzov
P. 139: 123rf.com © Margarita Borodina
P. 140: 123rf.com © Viorel Sima
P. 141: istockphoto.com © Viorika
Prikhodko
P. 141: 123rf.com © Oksana Kuzmina